UK JUICING FOR BEGINNERS

Juicing Handbook With Essential Healthy Juicing Recipes Using British Ingredients

With Metric Measurements

SUMMER G. FLORES

Copyright© 2023 By Summer G. Flores Rights Reserved

This book is copyright protected. It is only for personal use. You cannot amend, distribute, sell, use, quote or paraphrase any part of the content within this book, without the consent of the author or publisher.

Under no circumstances will any blame or legal responsibility be held against the publisher, or author, for any damages, reparation, or monetary loss due to the information contained within this book, either directly or indirectly.

Disclaimer Notice:

Please note the information contained within this document is for educational and entertainment purposes only. All effort has been executed to present accurate, up to date, reliable, complete information. No warranties of any kind are declared or implied. Readers acknowledge that the author is not engaged in the rendering of legal, financial, medical or professional advice. The content within this book has been derived from various sources. Please consult a licensed professional before attempting any techniques outlined in this book.

By reading this document, the reader agrees that under no circumstances is the author responsible for any losses, direct or indirect, that are incurred as a result of the use of the information contained within this document, including, but not limited to, errors, omissions, or inaccuracies.

EDITOR: LYN	**INTERIOR DESIGN: FAIZAN**
COVER ART: ABR	**FOOD STYLIST: JO**

Table of Contents

Introduction	1
Chapter 1	
A Brief Overview of Juicing	2
What Is Juicing	3
Why Juice	3
Juices Vs. Smoothies	5
Recommendations for Safe Juicing	6
Chapter 2	
How To Get Started	7
Tips of Selecting a Juicer	8
Foods For Juicing	8
FAQS	9
Chapter 3	
Start Your Day Green	10
Healthy Green Juice	11
Healthy Morning Juice	11
Cucumber with Pear Green Juice	11
Watermelon with Kale Green Juice	12
Broccoli Watercress Green Juice	12
Gingered Green Juice with Lemon	13
Green Powerhouse Juice	13
Carrot with Ginger Green Power Juice	14
Herb with Super Green Juice	14
Clean And Green	15
Spinach with Fruity Green Juice	15
Spinach with Kale Tango Green Juice	16
Royal Broccoli with Courgette Green Juice	16
Green Dream	16
Chapter 4	
Fruit-Based Juices	17
Apple Cinnamon-Infused Water	18
Kiwi Orange-Infused Water	18
Blueberry with Pineapple Juice	18
Limey Kiwi with Orange Juice	18
Purple Peach & Berry Juice	19
Limey Jicama Fruit Juice	19
Berry Renewal Fruit Juice	19
Grapefruit-Spinach Cooler	19
Orange Tart	20
Blackberry Hydrator	20
Beet with Berry and Apple Juice	21
Summer Blackberry	21
Limey Cilantro Gazpacho Juice	22
Kiwi-Melon Refresher	22
Parsley with Limey Orange Juice	22
Kiwi and Sparkling Pineapple Juice	23
Lemony Mango with Rockmelon Juice	23
Chapter 5	
Vegetable-Based Juices	24
Cucumber Celery Juice	25
Radish and Spinach Juice	25
Swede Anise Juice	25
Parsley Power Punch	25

Aubergine Carrot Juice Recipe	26
Tummy Saver Cabbage Juice	26
Savory Satisfying Salad Juice	26
Summer Carrot Sipper	26
Juicy Avocado with Spirulina Juice	27
Gingered Radish with Juicy Spinach	27
Juicy Carrot Refresher	28
Pepper, Carrot, And Apple Blend	28
Apple-Ginger Cleaner	29
Parsley with Tomato Vegetable Juice	29
Juicy Chard with Lemony Cabbage	30
Cara Cara Carrot	30

Chapter 6
Cleansing And Detoxifying — 31

Good Greens	32
Green Elixir	32
Parsley and Cauliflower Cleanse	33
Pear and Mixed Berry Juice	33
Kale Pineapple Cleansing Juice	34
Collard Veggie Cleansing Juice	34
Good Morning	35
Head Start	35
Coconut Limeade with Cilantro Juice	35
Lemony Liver Detox Juice	35
Simple Cabbage And Fennel Blend	36
Ruby Carrot Cleansing Juice	36
Spicy Sweet Potato	36

Chapter 7
Heart Health — 37

Nitric Oxide Recharge	38
Golden Heart Beet Juice	38
Apple Berry Green Tea Juice with Spinach	38
Minty Cucumbers and Gingered Carrot Juice	39
5 Minute Cucumber Celery Limey Juice	39
Grape-Cabbage Cure	39
Tangy Chad with Beet Cucumber Juice	39
Cinnamon Berry and Gingered Spinach Juice	40
Strawberry-Cucumber Juice	40
Kale Celery Fruity Juice	40
Apple Berry Juice	40
Orange Pineapple Chili	40
Sweet Summer Quencher	41
Ginger Pear Celery Juice	41
Kale Orange Apple Green Juice	41
Grapefruit And Kohlrabi	41
Strawberry Tomato Juice	41

Chapter 8
Anti-Aging and Energizing Juices — 42

Chocolate Caramel	43
Sweet Potato Orange	43
10 Minute Healthy Ulcer Care Drink	43
Milky Pistachio Juice	44
Cardamom spiced Coconut Juice	44
Spinach Protein Juice	45
Nutmeg Spiced Avocado Juice	45
Sweet Dreams	45
Spring Has Sprung	45
Minted Raspberry Cocktail	46
Apple, Kohlrabi, And Kale Sipper	46
Green Paradise	46
Plum Good	46
Ginger Beet and Tangy Celery Juice	47
Asparagus Blended with Peppered Chard	47
Plum Cocktail	47
Cruciferous Grapefruit Blend	48
Fine And Dandy	48
Quick and Healthy Carrot Celery Juice	48
Tangy Celery and Chard with Pear	48

Chapter 9
Structure Support — 49

Morning Green Glory	50
Electrolyte Lemonade	50
Cleanse Assist	51
Ginger Blast	51
Immunity Plus	52
Aloe Cleanser	52
Good, Good, Good Digestion	53
Chlorophyll Boost	53
Epic Green Juice	54
Apple and Pear Mint Juice	54
Asparagus Apple and Celery Juice	55
Orange Rabbit	55
I Dream Of Green	55
Now And Zen Green Juice	56
Emerald Alkalizing Juice	56

Chapter 10
Immune Boosting Juices — 57

Limey Orange and Cucumber Juice	58
Vitamin C Celebration	58
Berry Good	59
Walk In The Park	59
Orange Potato Bliss	59
Call Me Sweetheart	59
Lemony Red Velvet	60
Super Detox Juice	60
Spinach with Purple Pineapple	60
Heavenly Kale	60
Brainy Cooler	61
Swiss Plum	61
Tummy Tamer	61

Appendix 1 Measurement Conversion Chart	**62**
Appendix 2 The Dirty Dozen and Clean Fifteen	**63**
Appendix 3 Index	**64**

Introduction

As a female chef, I am a firm believer in the power of fresh juices. There's nothing quite like a glass of cold-pressed, nutrient-rich juice to kickstart your day and energize your body. I love experimenting with different combinations of fruits and vegetables, from tangy citrus to leafy greens and everything in between. Juicing allows me to create delicious and healthy drinks that are packed with vitamins, minerals, and antioxidants, making it an essential part of my daily routine. Whether you're looking to boost your immune system, detox your body, or simply enjoy a refreshing and flavorful beverage, juicing is a great way to do it. So why not try it out for yourself and see how it can transform your health and wellness?

Chapter 1
A Brief Overview of Juicing

What Is Juicing

Juicing is a fantastic way to get more fruits and vegetables into your diet. It involves extracting the juice from fresh produce using a juicer or blender. The resulting juice is packed with nutrients, vitamins, and minerals that are easily absorbed by your body. If you're new to juicing, it's essential to understand some basic principles to get the most out of your experience.

First and foremost, it's essential to choose the right fruits and vegetables. Dark leafy greens like kale, spinach, and collard greens are excellent sources of vitamins A, C, and K, while sweet fruits like apples, pears, and pineapple can add natural sweetness to your juice. For example, you could make a green juice using kale, cucumber, celery, lemon, and green apple for a healthy and refreshing drink.

Next, it's essential to invest in a good quality juicer or blender. A masticating juicer is the best option as it gently grinds and squeezes the juice from the produce, preserving its nutrients and enzymes. A high-speed blender can also work well for smoothies, but it may not extract as much juice as a juicer.

Lastly, it's essential to store your juice properly. Freshly made juice should be consumed immediately, but if you need to store it, keep it in an airtight container in the refrigerator for up to 24 hours. To prevent oxidation, add a little lemon juice or vitamin C powder to your juice before storing it.

In conclusion, juicing is an easy and convenient way to add more fruits and vegetables to your diet. By choosing the right produce, investing in a good quality juicer or blender, and storing your juice properly, you can create delicious and nutritious drinks that will help you look and feel your best.

Why Juice

Juicing has become increasingly popular over the years, and for good reason. There are many benefits to incorporating fresh juices into your diet. Here are some reasons why you should consider juicing:

PROVIDES A HIGH DOSE OF NUTRIENTS

Juicing allows you to consume a concentrated amount of vitamins, minerals, and antioxidants from fruits and vegetables in one glass of juice. This is especially helpful for people who struggle to eat the recommended daily intake of produce.

Research has shown that juicing can provide a concentrated dose of nutrients from fruits and vegetables. For example, a study published in the Journal of the Academy of Nutrition and Dietetics found that juicing kale, carrots, and celery increased the concentration of vitamin C, folate, and potassium compared to the raw vegetables. Similarly, a study published in the International Journal of Food Sciences and Nutrition found that juicing beetroot increased the concentration of nitrates, which are known to improve cardiovascular health.

In addition, juicing can help increase the bioavailability of nutrients in fruits and vegetables. A study published in the Journal of Agricultural and Food Chemistry found that juicing increased the availability of phenolic compounds in apples, which are known to have antioxidant and anti-inflammatory properties.
Promotes better digestion

Juicing can help improve digestion by providing fiber and enzymes that aid in digestion. This can lead to less bloating, gas, and constipation.

Several studies have shown that juicing can promote better digestion by providing fiber and enzymes that aid in digestion. For example, a study published in the Journal of Medicinal Food found that a juice made with ginger, lemon, and honey improved digestive symptoms in people with functional dyspepsia, a condition characterized by discomfort and pain in the upper digestive tract.

Another study published in the Journal of Food Science and Technology found that a juice made with papaya and pineapple improved digestion in healthy adults by increasing the activity of digestive enzymes. The enzymes in the juice helped break down proteins and carbohydrates, making them easier to digest.

Furthermore, juicing can provide a concentrated dose of fiber, which is essential for digestive health. A study published in the Journal of Functional Foods found that a juice made with kale, cucumber, and apple increased the concentration of dietary fiber compared to the raw vegetables. This increased fiber content can help promote regular bowel movements and reduce constipation.

BOOSTS IMMUNE SYSTEM

Juicing can help boost the immune system by providing essential vitamins and minerals that help support the body's defense against illness. Juicing can provide a range of nutrients that can help boost the immune system, including vitamins A, C, and E, as well as antioxidants and phytonutrients. For example, a study published in the Journal of Medicinal Food found that a juice made with beetroot, carrot, and ginger increased the concentration of vitamin C and total antioxidant capacity in healthy adults.

Another study published in the Journal of Nutrition and Metabolism found that a juice made with a combination of fruits and vegetables increased the concentration of immune-boosting compounds, such as beta-carotene, in healthy adults. This increased concentration of nutrients can help support the immune system and reduce the risk of illness.

In addition, juicing can help reduce inflammation, which is a contributing factor to many chronic diseases. A study published in the Journal of Clinical Biochemistry and Nutrition found that a juice made with ginger and turmeric reduced inflammation in healthy adults by decreasing the concentration of inflammatory markers in the blood.

INCREASES ENERGY LEVELS

Juicing can help increase energy levels by providing natural sugars and nutrients that the body can easily absorb. Juicing can provide a natural source of energy by delivering a concentrated dose of vitamins, minerals, and natural sugars that are easily absorbed by the body. For example, a study published in the Journal of the International Society of Sports Nutrition found that a juice made with beetroot improved exercise performance and increased energy levels in trained athletes by increasing the concentration of nitric oxide in the blood.

Similarly, a study published in the Journal of Chiropractic Medicine found that a juice made with a combination of fruits and vegetables improved energy levels and cognitive function in healthy adults. The increased energy levels were attributed to the natural sugars and nutrients found in the juice.

Juicing can also help support adrenal function, which plays a role in regulating energy levels. A study published in the Journal of the Academy of Nutrition and Dietetics found that a juice made with a combination of fruits and vegetables supported adrenal function in healthy adults, which can help increase energy levels.

AIDS IN WEIGHT LOSS

Juicing can be a helpful tool for weight loss by providing a low-calorie alternative to sugary drinks and snacks. Juicing can be a helpful tool for weight loss, but it should not be relied on as the sole method for losing weight. Juicing can help support weight loss by providing a concentrated dose of nutrients and fiber in a low-calorie form. For example, a study published in the journal "Nutrition" found that a juice made with a combination of fruits and vegetables helped overweight adults lose weight and improve their lipid profile.

However, it's important to note that juicing alone is not a sustainable or healthy way to lose weight in the long-term. Juicing can be low in protein, which is important for maintaining muscle mass and preventing muscle loss during weight loss. Additionally, juice diets that rely solely on juice and eliminate whole foods can be low in important nutrients like healthy fats and complex carbohydrates.

To use juicing as a tool for weight loss, it's important to incorporate it into a healthy and balanced diet that includes whole foods, lean protein, healthy fats, and complex carbohydrates. Juicing can be used as a supplement to increase nutrient intake and support weight loss, but it should not be relied on as the sole method for losing weight.

IMPROVES SKIN HEALTH

Juicing can help improve skin health by providing antioxidants that protect against skin damage caused by free radicals. Juicing can be a beneficial tool for improving skin health due to its ability to provide a range of nutrients that support skin function and repair. For example, a study published in the Journal of Agricultural and Food Chemistry found that a juice made with a combination of fruits and vegetables increased skin hydration and improved skin elasticity in healthy adults.

Juicing can also be a good source of antioxidants, which can help protect the skin from damage caused by free radicals. Free radicals are molecules that can damage cells and contribute to aging and disease. A study published in the Journal of Clinical and Aesthetic Dermatology found that a juice made with pomegranate and blueberries increased antioxidant activity in the blood, which can help protect the skin from damage.

Furthermore, juicing can provide a range of vitamins and minerals that are essential for skin health, such as vitamin C, vitamin E, and beta-carotene. These nutrients can help support collagen production, which is important for maintaining healthy and youthful-looking skin. A study published in the Journal of Investigative Dermatology found that vitamin C and E supplementation improved skin health and reduced the appearance of fine lines and wrinkles in healthy adults.

DETOXIFIES THE BODY

Juicing can help the body naturally detoxify by providing nutrients that support the liver and other detoxifying organs. Juicing can help the body naturally detoxify because it provides a concentrated dose of nutrients and antioxidants that support the body's natural detoxification processes. The liver is the primary organ responsible for detoxifying the body, and it requires a range of nutrients to function properly.

Juicing can provide a range of nutrients, such as vitamins, minerals, and antioxidants, that support liver function and help the body eliminate toxins. For example, a study published in the Journal of Medicinal Food found that a juice made with a combination of fruits and vegetables increased antioxidant activity in the blood and improved liver function in healthy adults.

Furthermore, juicing can provide a source of fiber, which is important for promoting regular bowel movements and eliminating waste from the body. A study published in the Journal of Nutrition found that a juice made with a combination of fruits and vegetables increased fecal output and improved bowel function in healthy adults.

Juicing can also help reduce the burden on the digestive system by providing nutrients in an easily digestible form. This can help free up energy for the body to focus on detoxification processes.

Overall, these studies suggest that juicing can help the body naturally detoxify by providing a concentrated dose of nutrients and antioxidants that support liver function and promote regular bowel movements.

Juices Vs. Smoothies

Juices and smoothies are both popular beverages that are made from fruits and vegetables, but there are some key differences between the two.

Juices are made by extracting the liquid from fruits and vegetables using a juicer, which removes the pulp and fiber. This results in a concentrated dose of nutrients and a lower calorie content compared to smoothies. Juices are typically consumed as a snack or supplement to a meal.

Smoothies, on the other hand, are made by blending fruits and vegetables with a liquid base, such as water, milk, or yogurt. The fiber is retained in the smoothie, which helps slow down digestion and provides a more sustained release of energy. Smoothies are often consumed as a meal replacement or a post-workout snack.

Here are some additional differences between juices and smoothies:
Nutrient density

Juices are typically more nutrient-dense than smoothies because they contain a concentrated amount of vitamins, minerals, and antioxidants. However, smoothies can provide a wider range of nutrients and fiber due to the inclusion of the pulp.

CALORIE CONTENT

Juices are lower in calories than smoothies because the fiber has been removed, which reduces the overall volume of the beverage. Smoothies can be higher in calories due to the inclusion of more ingredients and the retention of the fiber.

DIGESTION

Juices are easier to digest than smoothies because the fiber has been removed. This can be beneficial for people with digestive issues, but it can also cause blood sugar spikes if the juice contains a high amount of natural sugars. Smoothies can be slower to digest due to the inclusion of fiber, which can help promote satiety and prevent blood sugar spikes.

Ultimately, the choice between juices and smoothies depends on personal preference and health goals. Both can be nutritious and delicious additions to a healthy diet.

Recommendations for Safe Juicing

Here are some recommendations for safe juicing:

Choose fresh, high-quality produce: Use fresh, organic produce whenever possible to minimize exposure to pesticides and other chemicals. Wash all produce thoroughly before juicing.

Use a clean juicer: Clean your juicer thoroughly before and after each use to prevent the growth of harmful bacteria.

Don't juice certain foods: Avoid juicing certain foods, such as raw eggs, raw meat, and unpasteurized dairy products, as they may contain harmful bacteria that can cause foodborne illness.

Rotate your greens: Avoid juicing large amounts of the same greens, such as spinach or kale, every day. These greens contain oxalates, which can build up in the body and cause kidney stones over time.

Limit fruit intake: Fruits are high in natural sugars and can cause blood sugar spikes if consumed in excess. Aim to use no more than 1-2 servings of fruit per juice.

Store juice properly: Store fresh juice in an airtight container in the refrigerator and consume within 24-48 hours to minimize nutrient loss and reduce the risk of bacterial growth.

Consult with a healthcare professional: If you have any health conditions or are taking medication, consult with a healthcare professional before incorporating juicing into your diet.

By following these recommendations, you can safely incorporate juicing into your diet and reap the benefits of this nutritious and delicious practice.

Chapter 2
How To Get Started

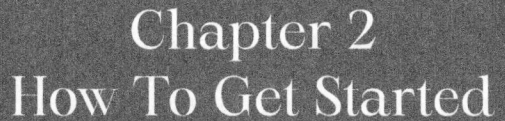

Tips of Selecting a Juicer

Type of juicer: There are several types of juicers, including centrifugal, masticating, and triturating. Centrifugal juicers are the most common and affordable, but they may not be as effective at juicing leafy greens. Masticating and triturating juicers are more expensive but can juice a wider variety of produce and produce a higher yield.

Ease of use and cleaning: Juicing can be a messy process, so it's important to choose a juicer that is easy to use and clean. Look for a juicer with dishwasher-safe parts or a simple cleaning process.

Yield and efficiency: Different juicers can produce different amounts of juice from the same amount of produce, so it's important to choose a juicer that produces a high yield and doesn't waste a lot of produce.

Noise level: Some juicers can be quite loud, so if you live in a small space or prefer a quieter environment, look for a juicer that produces less noise.

Price: Juicers can range in price from under $50 to over $500, so consider your budget when choosing a juicer.

Brand and customer reviews: Do some research on the brands and models you are considering, and read customer reviews to get an idea of their performance, durability, and overall satisfaction.

Foods For Juicing

FRUITS

Oranges: Oranges are high in vitamin C, which can help support immune function and skin health. They also contain folate and potassium.

Berries: Berries, such as blueberries, raspberries, and strawberries, are rich in antioxidants and anti-inflammatory compounds that can help protect against chronic disease. They also contain fiber and vitamin C.

Pineapple: Pineapple contains an enzyme called bromelain, which can help reduce inflammation and improve digestion. It also contains vitamin C and manganese.

Apples: Apples are a good source of fiber and vitamin C, and they contain flavonoids that may have anti-inflammatory and anti-cancer properties.

Grapes: Grapes contain antioxidants called polyphenols, which can help protect against oxidative stress and inflammation. They also contain vitamin C and fiber.

Kiwi: Kiwi is high in vitamin C and fiber, and it contains antioxidants that can help protect against oxidative stress and inflammation. It also contains enzymes that can aid in digestion.

Pomegranate: Pomegranate contains polyphenols and other antioxidants that can help protect against chronic disease. It also contains vitamin C and potassium.

Lemon: Lemon is a good source of vitamin C, and it contains compounds that can help improve digestion and support immune function.

VEGETABLES

Kale: Kale is a nutrient powerhouse, containing high levels of vitamins A, C, and K, as well as calcium and iron. It also contains antioxidants and anti-inflammatory compounds.

Carrots: Carrots are rich in beta-carotene, which is converted to vitamin A in the body. They also contain vitamin C, fiber, and other antioxidants that can help support immune function.

Beets: Beets are high in nitrates, which can help improve blood flow and lower blood pressure. They also contain betaine, a compound that may help protect against liver damage.

Spinach: Spinach is rich in iron, magnesium, and potassium, as well as vitamins A and C. It also contains antioxidants and anti-inflammatory compounds that may help protect against chronic disease.

Cucumber: Cucumber is a hydrating vegetable that is low in calories but high in fiber and vitamin K. It also contains antioxidants that can help protect against oxidative stress.

Celery: Celery is a good source of vitamin K and antioxidants, and it may help reduce inflammation and lower blood pressure.

Ginger: Ginger has anti-inflammatory and anti-nausea properties, and it may help alleviate muscle soreness and improve digestion.

HERBS, SPICES, AND MIX-INS

Turmeric: Turmeric contains a compound called curcumin, which has anti-inflammatory and antioxidant properties. It may also help improve brain function and reduce the risk of chronic disease.

Mint: Mint contains antioxidants and anti-inflammatory compounds, and it may help soothe digestive issues and alleviate nausea.

Cinnamon: Cinnamon contains antioxidants and anti-inflammatory compounds, and it may help improve blood sugar control and reduce the risk of heart disease.

Chia Seeds: Chia seeds are a good source of fiber and omega-3 fatty acids, and they can help promote satiety and support digestive health.

Coconut Water: Coconut water is a natural source of electrolytes, which can help rehydrate the body after exercise or illness.

FAQS

Is juicing a healthy way to consume fruits and vegetables?

Yes, juicing can be a healthy way to consume fruits and vegetables, as it allows you to easily and quickly consume a variety of nutrient-rich produce. However, it's important to also consume whole fruits and vegetables in your diet to ensure you are getting adequate fiber.

CAN JUICING BE HARMFUL?

While juicing can provide many health benefits, it's important to practice safe juicing habits and not rely solely on juice for your nutrition. Overconsumption of certain juices, such as beet juice, can cause digestive issues or other health problems. It's also important to ensure your juicing equipment is properly cleaned to prevent the growth of harmful bacteria.

CAN I JUICE ANY FRUIT OR VEGETABLE?

While most fruits and vegetables can be juiced, some may not be suitable or may have an unpleasant taste when juiced. It's important to research and experiment with different produce to find the combinations that work best for you.

Chapter 3
Start Your Day Green

Healthy Green Juice
Prep time: 5 minutes | Cook time: 10 minutes | Serves 2

- 2 green apples, halved
- 4 stalks celery, leaves removed
- 1 cucumber
- 6 leaves kale
- ½ lemon, peeled
- 1 (1-inch) piece fresh ginger

1. Thoroughly wash all ingredients, cut and prepare them.
2. Use a juicer to extract the juice from the ingredients.
3. Pour the juice into a glass and enjoy.

Healthy Morning Juice
Prep time: 5 minutes | Cook time: 10 minutes | Serves 2

- 3 medium carrots, cut into chunks
- 2-3 leaves of kale, roughly chopped
- 3 stalks of celery, roughly chopped
- 2-3 medium apples, cut into chunks

1. Wash the kale, celery, apples, and carrots.
2. Use a juicer to extract the juice from the ingredients.
3. Pour the juice into two glasses.
4. Add 1-2 ice cubes (if desired) and enjoy.

Cucumber with Pear Green Juice
Prep time: 10 minutes | Cook time: 0 minutes | Serves 1

- 1 cup spinach
- 2 cups green beans
- 1 cucumber
- ½ pear
- ½ lemon

1. Wash all the ingredients.
2. Trim the ends from the green beans and cucumber, then cut into 10 cm pieces.
3. Cut the pear into quarters, removing the core and seeds, but leaving the skin intact.
4. Peel the lemon half and cut into quarters.
5. Place a jug under the juicer's spout to collect the juice.
6. Feed each ingredient through the juicer's intake tube in the order listed.
7. When the juice stops flowing, remove the jug and stir the juice.
8. Serve immediately.

Watermelon with Kale Green Juice

Prep time: 5 minutes | **Cook time:** 0 minutes | **Serves 1**

- 1½ cups watermelon
- 4 kale leaves
- ½ lime
- 2 celery stalks

1. Wash the kale, lime, and celery.
2. Cut the watermelon into quarters. Remove the rind and discard. Cut the watermelon into smaller pieces.
3. Trim the ends from the celery, then cut into 10 cm pieces.
4. Peel the lime half and cut into quarters.
5. Place a jug under the juicer's spout to collect the juice.
6. Feed each ingredient through the juicer's intake tube in the order listed.
7. When the juice stops flowing, remove the jug and stir the juice.
8. Serve immediately.

Broccoli Watercress Green Juice

Prep time: 5 minutes | **Cook time:** 0 minutes | **Serves 1**

- 2 cups spinach
- 1 cup clover sprouts
- 1 cup watercress
- 2 green apples
- 2 cups broccoli

1. Wash all the ingredients thoroughly.
2. Remove the apple cores and discard. Cut the apples into quarters, leaving the peel intact.
3. Remove the stalk from the broccoli crown with a knife and discard or save to juice later. Cut the crown into small florets.
4. Place a jug or glass under the juicer's spout to collect the juice.
5. Feed each ingredient through the juicer's intake tube in the order listed.
6. When the juice stops flowing, remove the jug or glass and stir the juice.
7. Serve immediately.

Gingered Green Juice with Lemon
Prep time: 15 minutes | Cook time: 0 minutes | Serves 2

- 2 Fresh green apples cut into halves
- 2 Fresh celery stalks with their leaves removed
- 1 Fresh cucumber, skin peeled off
- 4-5 Fresh kale leaves
- ½ a fresh lemon (peel off the skin)
- A small piece of fresh ginger

1. Take all the fresh ingredients. Peel and chop them coarsely.
2. Now, put all these ingredients in a juicer. Extract the green juice and keep it in a large container.
3. Then serve in glasses and top the glasses with some more grated ginger and a bit of lime juice.
4. Enjoy!

Green Powerhouse Juice
Prep time: 15 minutes | Cook time: 0 minutes | Serves 2

- 4 fresh beetroot, peeled and chopped into bite-sized pieces
- 2 fresh celery stalks with their leaves removed
- 1 fresh cucumber, skin peeled off and sliced
- 1 bunch fresh spinach
- ½ a fresh lemon (peel off the skin)
- A small piece of fresh ginger

1. Wash all the fresh ingredients.
2. Peel and chop them into bite-sized pieces.
3. Put all these ingredients in a juicer and extract the juice.
4. Keep the green juice in a large container.
5. Pour the juice into glasses and add some more grated ginger, a bit of lime juice and a slice of cucumber on top.
6. Serve immediately.
7. Enjoy!

Carrot with Ginger Green Power Juice
Prep time: 5 minutes | Cook time: 0 minutes | Serves 1

- 2 stalks celery
- 2 small apples
- 2 carrots
- 5 small radishes
- 1 small piece ginger
- 1 cup spinach

1. Wash the celery, apples, carrots, radishes, spinach, and ginger.
2. Cut the ingredients into chunks and add them to a juicer.
3. Extract the juice and pour it into a glass.
4. Stir the juice well before drinking.
5. Enjoy your refreshing green juice!

Herb with Super Green Juice
Prep time: 5 minutes | Cook time: 0 minutes | Serves 1

- 2 leaves Swiss chard
- 1 cup kale ½ small beet
- ½ cup pineapple, chopped
- 2 medium green apples, chopped
- 1 sprig fresh mint
- ½ medium lemon, peeled

1. Wash the herbs and greens under running water, making sure to remove any dirt or debris.
2. Chop the vegetables and fruit into small pieces and add them to a juicer along with the sprig of fresh mint.
3. Process the ingredients and pour the juice into a tall glass.
4. Stir well and serve immediately. Enjoy your delicious and nutritious green juice!

Clean And Green

Prep time: 5 minutes | Cook time: 10 minutes| Serves 2

- 4-inch piece broccoli stem
- 4 large Swiss chard leaves
- 1 medium apple
- 2 large celery stalks

1. Feed the ingredients one at a time, in the order listed, through the juicer.
2. Stir the juice and pour into glasses to serve.

Spinach with Fruity Green Juice

Prep time: 5 minutes | Cook time: 0 minutes | Serves 2

- 1 bunch spinach leaves
- 1 medium apple
- 1 medium pear
- 1 medium navel orange

1. Peel, core, and chop the apple and pear as needed.
2. Cut the navel orange into segments and remove any seeds.
3. Place a container under the juicer's spout.
4. Feed the ingredients one at a time, in the order listed, through the juicer.
5. Stir the juice and pour into glasses to serve.

Spinach with Kale Tango Green Juice
Prep time: 5 minutes | Cook time: 0 minutes | Serves 2

- 4 large kale leaves
- 3 large stalks celery
- 1 ripe mango
- 1 small bunch spinach leaves

1. Prepare the ingredients by washing, peeling, and cutting them as needed.
2. Place a jug or container under the juicer's spout.
3. Feed each ingredient one at a time through the juicer, in the order listed.
4. Stir the juice and pour into glasses to serve.

Royal Broccoli with Courgette Green Juice
Prep time: 5 minutes | Cook time: 0 minutes | Serves 1

- ½ head broccoli
- 4 leaves kale
- ½ green bell pepper
- 1 courgette, peeled
- 1 green apple

1. Wash the pepper, broccoli, courgette, kale, and apple and cut into chunks.
2. Then pass all ingredients through a juicer.
3. Pour the juice into a glass and drink immediately.

Green Dream
Prep time: 5 minutes | Cook time: 10 minutes | Serves 2

- 3 stalks celery
- 2/3 cucumber
- 1 cup broccoli
- 2 green apples
- ½ lemon

1. Wash the celery, cucumber, broccoli, apples, and lemon and run through a juicer.
2. Pour the juice into a glass, stir well, and enjoy.

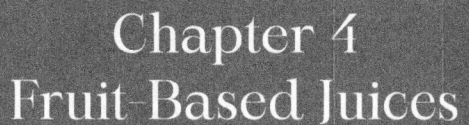

Chapter 4
Fruit-Based Juices

Apple Cinnamon Infused Water
Prep time: 5 minutes | Cook time: 10 minutes | Serves 2

- 250ml water
- ¼ medium tart green apple (such as Granny Smith), cored and thinly sliced
- ½ teaspoon fresh lemon juice
- ⅛ teaspoon ground cinnamon
- 7 drops liquid stevia
- 120ml ice cubes

1. Add all ingredients to a glass.
2. Serve.

Blueberry with Pineapple Juice
Prep time: 5 minutes | Cook time: 0 minutes | Serves 2

- 350g blueberries
- 250g pineapple
- 1 medium apple

1. Peel, cut, deseed, and/or chop the ingredients as needed.
2. Place a container under the juicer's spout.
3. Feed the ingredients one at a time, in the order listed, through the juicer.
4. Stir the juice and pour into glasses to serve.

Kiwi Orange Infused Water
Prep time: 5 minutes | Cook time: 10 minutes | Serves 2

- 250 ml water
- 3 slices fresh orange
- ½ medium kiwi, peeled and sliced
- ½ cup ice cubes

1. Fill a pitcher or a glass with water.
2. Add the sliced orange and kiwi to the water.
3. Stir the mixture to allow the flavors to infuse.
4. Add ice cubes to the glass or pitcher.
5. Chill for 10-15 minutes before serving.

Limey Kiwi with Orange Juice
Prep time: 5 minutes | Cook time: 0 minutes | Serves 2

- 3 medium navel oranges
- 3 ripe kiwis
- 1 teaspoon lime zest

1. Peel, cut, deseed, and/or chop the ingredients as needed.
2. Place a container under the juicer's spout.
3. Feed the oranges and kiwis through the juicer.
4. Stir the lime zest into the juice and pour into glasses to serve.

Purple Peach & Berry Juice
Prep time: 5 minutes | Cook time: 0 minutes | Serves 2

- 2 medium peaches
- 1 medium apple
- 1 cup blueberries
- 1 cup parsley leaves

1. Peel, cut, deseed, and/or chop the ingredients as needed.
2. Place a container under the juicer's spout.
3. Feed the ingredients one at a time, in the order listed, through the juicer.
4. Stir the juice and pour into glasses to serve.

Limey Jicama Fruit Juice
Prep time: 5 minutes | Cook time: 0 minutes | Serves 2

- 560g jicama
- 2 medium carrots
- 1 medium pear
- ½ lemon
- ½ lime

1. Peel, cut, deseed, and/or chop the ingredients as needed.
2. Place a container under the juicer's spout.
3. Feed the ingredients one at a time, in the order listed, through the juicer.
4. Stir the juice and pour into glasses to serve.

Berry Renewal Fruit Juice
Prep time: 5 minutes | Cook time: 0 minutes | Serves 2

- 2 cups raspberries
- 1 large carrot
- 1 medium pear
- 1 tablespoon freshly squeezed lemon juice

1. Wash, peel, cut, and/or chop the ingredients as needed.
2. Place a container under the juicer's spout.
3. Feed the raspberries, carrot, and pear through the juicer.
4. Stir the lemon juice into the juice and pour into glasses to serve.

Grapefruit-Spinach Cooler
Prep time: 5 minutes | Cook time: 10 minutes | Serves 2

- Handful spinach
- 1 large pink or red grapefruit, peeled
- 1 large cucumber

1. Feed the ingredients one at a time, in the order listed, through the juicer.
2. Stir the juice and pour into glasses to serve.

Orange Tart

Prep time: 5 minutes | Cook time: 10 minutes | Serves 2

- 2 blood oranges, peeled
- 1-inch piece fresh ginger root
- 1 large lemon
- 2 large celery stalks
- ½ cup fresh coconut water

1. Feed the ingredients one at a time, in the order listed, through the juicer.
2. Stir the juice and pour into glasses to serve.

Blackberry Hydrator

Prep time: 5 minutes | Cook time: 10 minutes | Serves 2

- 2 cups blackberries
- 2 firm pears
- 8 medium celery stalks

1. Feed the ingredients one at a time, in the order listed, through the juicer.
2. Stir the juice and pour into glasses to serve.

Beet with Berry and Apple Juice
Prep time: 5 minutes | Cook time: 0 minutes | Serves 2

- 2 cups mixed berries (such as raspberries, blueberries, and blackberries)
- 2 small beets
- 1 small apple

1. Peel, cut, deseed, and/or chop the ingredients as needed.
2. Place a container under the juicer's spout.
3. Feed the ingredients one at a time, in the order listed, through the juicer.
4. Stir the juice and pour into glasses to serve.

Summer Blackberry
Prep time: 5 minutes | Cook time: 10 minutes| Serves 2

- 4 medium kale leaves
- 4 small celery stalks
- 1 cup blackberries
- 12 parsley sprigs
- 2 large romaine leaves
- 1 small apple

1. Feed the ingredients one at a time, in the order listed, through the juicer.
2. Stir the juice and pour into glasses to serve.

Limey Cilantro Gazpacho Juice
Prep time: 5 minutes | Cook time: 0 minutes | Serves 2

- 2 ripe vine tomatoes
- 1 ripe mango
- ½ small orange bell pepper
- ½ lime
- 3 sprigs coriander

1. Peel, chop, deseed, and/or slice the ingredients as necessary.
2. Place a container beneath the juicer's spout.
3. Feed the ingredients through the juicer in the order listed.
4. Stir the juice and pour into glasses to serve.

Kiwi-Melon Refresher
Prep time: 5 minutes | Cook time: 10 minutes | Serves 2

- 2 large bok choy stems
- 2 kiwifruit
- 1 cup watermelon

1. Feed the ingredients one at a time, in the order listed, through the juicer.
2. Stir the juice and pour into glasses to serve.

Parsley with Limey Orange Juice
Prep time: 5 minutes | Cook time: 0 minutes | Serves 2

- 1 medium sweet orange
- 1 medium apple
- 1 medium pear
- ½ bunch flat-leaf parsley
- ½ lime

1. Peel, core, and/or chop the ingredients as needed.
2. Place a container under the juicer's spout.
3. Feed the ingredients one at a time, in the order listed, through the juicer.
4. Stir the juice and pour into glasses to serve.

Kiwi and Sparkling Pineapple Juice
Prep time: 5 minutes | Cook time: 0 minutes | Serves 2

- 1 small pineapple
- 3 ripe kiwis
- 1 cup sparkling water

1. Peel, cut, deseed, and/or chop the ingredients as needed.
2. Place a container under the juicer's spout.
3. Feed the pineapple and kiwis through the juicer.
4. Pour the juice into glasses and stir in the sparkling water. Serve immediately.

Lemony Mango with Rockmelon Juice
Prep time: 5 minutes | Cook time: 0 minutes | Serves 2

- 2 ripe mangoes
- 2 cups watermelon
- 1 cup rockmelon1 tablespoon freshly squeezed lemon juice

1. Peel, cut, deseed, and/or chop the ingredients as needed.
2. Place a container under the juicer's spout.
3. Feed the mangoes, watermelon, and rockmelon through the juicer.
4. Stir the lemon juice into the juice and pour into glasses to serve.

Chapter 5
Vegetable-Based Juices

Cucumber Celery Juice
Prep time: 5 minutes | Cook time: 10 minutes| Serves 2

- 2 large stalks celery
- 1 small head broccoli
- 1 cucumber
- 1 small pear
- ½ bunch parsley leaves

1. Peel, trim and chop the ingredients as needed.
2. Place a container under the juicer's spout.
3. Feed the ingredients one at a time, in the order listed, through the juicer.
4. Stir the juice and pour into glasses to serve.

Radish and Spinach Juice
Prep time: 5 minutes | Cook time: 10 minutes| Serves 2

- 8 small radishes with greens
- 2 cups baby spinach leaves
- 1 large carrot
- 1 large stalk celery
- 1 medium apple
- ½-inch piece ginger root

1. Peel, cut, deseed, and/or chop the ingredients as needed.
2. Place a container under the juicer's spout.
3. Feed the ingredients one at a time, in the order listed, through the juicer.
4. Stir the juice and pour into glasses to serve.

Swede Anise Juice
Prep time: 8 minutes | Cook time: 0 minutes | Serves 2

- ½ Swede raw/mashed
- 1 Apple raw
- 3 Carrots medium raw
- ¼ Anise bulb medium raw

1. With the help of a power juicer, convert the above ingredients into juice. If the swede is highly waxed, then remove the outer skin before introducing it into the juicer.
2. Serve with some ice cubes.
3. Enjoy!

Parsley Power Punch
Prep time: 5 minutes | Cook time: 0 minutes | Serves 2

- 1 large bunch flat-leaf parsley
- 1 Apple, cored and sliced
- 2 Carrots, peeled and sliced
- 1 stalk celery, sliced

1. You will require a good juicer. If you have a centrifugal juicer, then push the parsley into the juicer with celery or carrots to get a good yield.
2. The apple should be introduced to the juicer last to obtain all the nutrients.
3. Stir the juice and pour into glasses over ice cubes to serve.
4. Enjoy!

Aubergine Carrot Juice Recipe

Prep time: 5 minutes | Cook time: 0 minutes | Serves 2

- 1 Aubergine raw
- 3 Carrots raw
- 2 Apples raw
- 1 Celery stalk raw

1. Juice up the whole aubergine with the skin and the seeds.
2. Then juice up the other ingredients and pour it into a glass and serve.
3. Enjoy!

Tummy Saver Cabbage Juice

Prep time: 6 minutes | Cook time: 0 minutes | Serves 2

- ½ Head of cabbage raw
- 1 celery raw
- 2 Carrots raw
- 2 Apples raw

1. After washing, push the vegetables into a power juicer and prepare the juice.
2. Pour it into a glass and serve. Make sure to drink it soon after juicing within a couple of minutes.
3. Enjoy!

Savory Satisfying Salad Juice

Prep time: 10 minutes | Cook time: 0 minutes | Serves 2

- 1 handful of Spinach
- 3 medium sized Tomatoes
- 2 whole Spring Onions
- 2 sticks of Celery
- 2 large Carrots
- 1 Red pepper (capsicum)
- 1 teaspoon Olive oil (cold-pressed)
- Pepper and sea salt to taste

1. Wash all the ingredients under running water. De-seed capsicum thoroughly; chop all the components as per size fitting to juicer jar.
2. Combine all the ingredients and juice until smooth.
3. Lastly, add olive oil and season with sea salt and pepper if desired. Green or yellow bell pepper can also be taken in place of red bell pepper.
4. Enjoy!

Summer Carrot Sipper

Prep time: 5 minutes | Cook time: 10 minutes | Serves 2

- 2 large carrots
- 2 large kale leaves
- ½ red apple
- 1 cup watermelon

1. Feed the ingredients one at a time, in the order listed, through the juicer.
2. Stir the juice and pour into glasses to serve.

Juicy Avocado with Spirulina Juice

Prep time: 10 minutes | Cook time: 0 minutes | Serves 2

- 2 small apples
- 1 seedless cucumber
- 1 ripe avocado
- 1 teaspoon spirulina powder

1. Peel, cut, deseed, and/or chop the ingredients as needed.
2. Place a container under the juicer's spout.
3. Feed the apples and cucumber through the juicer.
4. In a blender or food processor, blend the avocado until smooth.
5. Stir the pureed avocado and spirulina into the juice and pour into glasses to serve.

Gingered Radish with Juicy Spinach

Prep time: 5 minutes | Cook time: 0 minutes | Serves 2

- 8 small radishes with greens
- 2 cups baby spinach leaves
- 1 large carrot
- 1 large stalk celery
- 1 medium apple
- 1.25cm piece gingerroot

1. Peel, cut, deseed, and/or chop the ingredients as needed.
2. Place a container under the juicer's spout.
3. Feed the ingredients one at a time, in the order listed, through the juicer.
4. Stir the juice and pour into glasses to serve.

Juicy Carrot Refresher

Prep time: 5 minutes | Cook time: 0 minutes | Serves 2

- 5 medium carrots
- 3 medium green apples
- 1 large red bell pepper

1. Peel, cut, deseed, and/or chop the ingredients as needed.
2. Place a container under the juicer's spout.
3. Feed the ingredients one at a time, in the order listed, through the juicer.
4. Stir the juice and pour into glasses to serve.
5. Enjoy!

Pepper, Carrot, And Apple Blend

Prep time: 5 minutes | Cook time: 10 minutes | Serves 2

- 1 green bell pepper
- 4 large carrots
- 1 small apple

1. Feed the ingredients one at a time, in the order listed, through the juicer.
2. Stir the juice and pour into glasses to serve.

Apple-Ginger Cleaner
Prep time: 5 minutes | Cook time: 10 minutes| Serves 2

- 1 small lemon
- 1-inch piece fresh ginger root
- 1 medium apple
- 1 cup fresh coconut water

1. Feed the ingredients one at a time, in the order listed, through the juicer.
2. Stir the juice and pour into glasses to serve.

Parsley with Tomato Vegetable Juice
Prep time: 5 minutes | Cook time: 0 minutes | Serves 4

- 6 red radishes with greens
- 3 plum tomatoes
- 2 medium beets
- 2 small carrots
- 2 large stalks celery
- 2 cups packed parsley leaves

1. Peel, cut, deseed, and/or chop the ingredients as needed.
2. Place a container under the juicer's spout.
3. Feed the ingredients one at a time, in the order listed, through the juicer.
4. Stir the juice and pour into glasses to serve.

Juicy Chard with Lemony Cabbage
Prep time: 5 minutes | Cook time: 0 minutes | Serves 4

- 4 large Swiss chard leaves
- 2 large carrots
- 1 medium apple
- ¼ small head red cabbage
- 2 tablespoons freshly squeezed lemon juice

1. Wash all the vegetables under running water. Peel and chop the carrots and apple as needed.
2. Place a container under the juicer's spout.
3. Feed the Swiss chard, carrots, apple, and cabbage through the juicer.
4. Stir the lemon juice into the juice and pour into glasses to serve.

Cara Cara Carrot
Prep time: 5 minutes | Cook time: 10 minutes | Serves 2

- 2 large carrots
- 8 parsley sprigs
- 2 Cara Cara or other small oranges, peeled
- 1 small red apple

1. Feed the ingredients one at a time, in the order listed, through the juicer.
2. Stir the juice and pour into glasses to serve.

Chapter 6
Cleansing And Detoxifying

Good Greens

Prep time: 5 minutes | Cook time: 10 minutes | Makes about 12 ounces

- 2 small mustard green leaves
- 2 large kale leaves
- 2 Swiss chard leaves
- 1 small lime, peeled
- ½ large cucumber

1. Feed the ingredients one at a time, in the order listed, through the juicer.
2. Stir the juice and pour into glasses to serve.

Green Elixir

Prep time: 5 minutes | Cook time: 10 minutes | Serves 2

- 10 kale leaves
- 2 large cucumbers
- 1 fennel bulb, plus fronds
- 4 pears
- 4 celery sticks

1. Wash and prepare the ingredients, and cut to size for your juicer.
2. Run through your juicer, then pour into a glass and enjoy.

Parsley and Cauliflower Cleanse
Prep time: 10 minutes | Cook time: 0 minutes | Serves 2

- 250g cauliflower
- 1 firm pear
- 8 sprigs of parsley
- 4 large celery stalks

1. Peel, cut, deseed, and/or chop the ingredients as needed.
2. Place a container under the juicer's spout.
3. Feed the ingredients in the order listed, through the juicer.
4. Alternate ingredients, finishing with the celery.
5. Stir the juice and pour into glasses to serve.

Pear and Mixed Berry Juice
Prep time: 10 minutes | Cook time: 0 minutes | Serves 2

- 1 cup mixed berries (such as strawberries, raspberries, and blueberries)
- 1 firm pear
- 4 cups spinach
- 4 medium celery stalks

1. Wash and prepare the ingredients, and cut to size for your juicer.
2. Feed the berries and pear through the juicer first, followed by the spinach and celery.
3. Stir the juice and pour into glasses to serve.

Kale Pineapple Cleansing Juice
Prep time: 5 minutes | Cook time: 0 minutes | Serves 2

- 4 kale leaves
- 2 cups pineapple

1. Peel, chop or deseed the ingredients as needed.
2. Place a container under the juicer's spout.
3. Feed the ingredients in the listed order through the juicer.
4. Alternate the ingredients, finishing with the pineapple.
5. Stir the juice and pour it into glasses to serve.

Collard Veggie Cleansing Juice
Prep time: 15 minutes | Cook time: 0 minutes | Serves 2

- 1 red bell pepper
- 2 large carrots
- 1 small collard leaf
- 1 medium kale leaf
- ½ large cucumber
- Handful coriander or parsley
- 1 medium red apple

1. Prepare the ingredients by washing and cutting them into pieces that will fit your juicer.
2. Place a container under the juicer's spout.
3. Feed the ingredients in the order listed, through the juicer.
4. Alternate ingredients, finishing with the apple.
5. Stir the juice and pour into glasses to serve.

Good Morning
Prep time: 5 minutes | Cook time: 10 minutes | Serves 2

- 1 orange or red bell pepper
- 2 large carrots
- 1 pink or red grapefruit, peeled

1. Feed the ingredients one at a time, in the order listed, through the juicer.
2. Stir the juice and pour into glasses to serve.

Head Start
Prep time: 5 minutes | Cook time: 10 minutes | Serves 2

- 1-inch piece fresh ginger root
- 2 large carrots
- 1 small zucchini
- ½ lemon
- 1 firm pear
- 1 medium apple

1. Feed the ingredients one at a time, in the order listed, through the juicer.
2. Stir the juice and pour into glasses to serve.

Coconut Limeade with Cilantro Juice
Prep time: 10 minutes | Cook time: 0 minutes | Serves 2

- 1/4 medium lemon
- 1/4 medium lime, peeled
- 1-inch piece fresh ginger root
- Handful cilantro
- 1-pound carrots
- 1/2 cup fresh coconut water

1. Peel, cut, deseed, and/or chop the ingredients as needed.
2. Place a container under the juicer's spout.
3. Feed the ingredients in the order listed, through the juicer.
4. Alternate ingredients, finishing with the carrots.
5. Stir the coconut water directly into the juice.

Lemony Liver Detox Juice
Prep time: 10 minutes | Cook time: 0 minutes | Serves 2

- 1 small baby pak choi
- 3 large kale leaves
- 1 medium apple
- 1 small lemon
- ½-inch piece ginger root

1. Peel, cut, deseed, and/or chop the ingredients as needed.
2. Place a container under the juicer's spout.
3. Feed the ingredients one at a time, in the order listed, through the juicer.
4. Stir the juice and pour into glasses to serve.

Simple Cabbage And Fennel Blend
Prep time: 5 minutes | Cook time: 10 minutes| Serves 2

- 2 cups red cabbage
- 2 small fennel bulbs

1. Feed the ingredients one at a time, in the order listed, through the juicer.
2. Stir the juice and pour into glasses to serve.

Ruby Carrot Cleansing Juice
Prep time: 10 minutes | Cook time: 0 minutes | Serves 1

- 1 large beetroot, cut into slices
- 1 inch piece of ginger
- 2 large carrots
- 1 large apple
- 2 thick slices peeled, and de-seeded cucumbers

1. To prepare this recipe, use a juicer to carefully process the beetroot slices.
2. Follow with ginger, carrots, apple, and finally the cucumber slices.
3. This drink will help to detox your body by providing plenty of fibre that is particularly abundant in the beetroot.
4. The ginger acts as a natural healer and can help you feel calm and collected, which is essential for any journey to well-being, detoxification, and weight loss.

Spicy Sweet Potato
Prep time: 5 minutes | Cook time: 10 minutes| Serves 2

- 2-inch piece fresh ginger root
- 2-inch piece fresh turmeric root
- 1 small sweet potato, peeled
- ½ orange, red, or yellow bell pepper
- 2 cups spinach
- 1 large cucumber

1. Feed the ingredients one at a time, in the order listed, through the juicer.
2. Stir the juice and pour into glasses to serve.

Chapter 7
Heart Health

Nitric Oxide Recharge

Prep time: 5 minutes | Cook time: 10 minutes | Serves 2

- Handful rocket (arugula)
- 4-inch piece broccoli stalk
- 4 large carrots
- 1 orange, peeled
- 4 large celery stalks

1. Thoroughly wash all ingredients, chop and run through a juicer.
2. Pour into glasses and serve.

Golden Heart Beet Juice

Prep time: 5 minutes | Cook time: 10 minutes | Serves 2

- 6 medium carrots
- ¼ lemon
- 1 orange, peeled ½ golden or red beetroot
- 1 medium red apple

1. Thoroughly wash all ingredients, chop and run through a juicer.
2. Pour into glasses and serve.

Apple Berry Green Tea Juice with Spinach

Prep time: 5 minutes | Cook time: 0 minutes | Serves 1

- 180ml green tea
- 2 cups spinach
- 1 red apple
- 2 teaspoons ground flaxseed

1. Brew the green tea and let it cool.
2. Wash the spinach and apple.
3. Remove the apple core and discard. Cut the apple into quarters, leaving the peel intact.
4. Place a pitcher under the juicer's spout to collect the juice.
5. Feed the spinach, then the apple through the juicer's intake tube.
6. When the juice stops flowing, remove the pitcher, add the green tea and flaxseed, then stir.
7. Serve immediately.

Minty Cucumbers and Gingered Carrot Juice

Prep time: 5 minutes | Cook time: 0 minutes | Serves 1

- 2 cucumbers
- 3 carrots
- 2 tablespoons parsley
- 1 sprig of mint leaves Fresh ginger root

1. Wash all the ingredients. Place a jug under the juicer's spout to collect the juice.
2. Feed each ingredient through the juicer's intake tube in the order listed.
3. When the juice stops flowing, remove the jug and stir the juice.
4. Serve immediately.

5 Minute Cucumber Celery Limey Juice

Prep time: 5 minutes | Cook time: 0 minutes | Serves 1

- 1 cucumber
- 1 romaine lettuce heart
- 4 celery sticks
- 1 lime
- ½ tablespoon wheatgrass powder

1. Wash the cucumber, romaine lettuce, celery, and lime.
2. Peel the lime and cut into quarters.
3. Place a jug under the juicer's spout to collect the juice.
4. Feed the first four ingredients through the juicer's intake tube in the order listed.
5. Serve immediately.

Grape-Cabbage Cure

Prep time: 5 minutes | Cook time: 10 minutes | Serves 2

- 1 cup red cabbage
- 2 cups black, purple, or red grapes
- 12 parsley sprigs
- 1 medium apple

1. Feed the ingredients one at a time, in the order listed, through the juicer.
2. Stir the juice and pour into glasses to serve.

Tangy Chad with Beet Cucumber Juice

Prep time: 5 minutes | Cook time: 0 minutes | Serves 1

- 1 cucumber
- 1 Swiss chard leaf
- 2 sprigs of coriander
- ½ small to medium-sized beetroot
- 3 celery sticks
- ½ lemon Fresh ginger root

1. Wash all the ingredients.
2. Remove any greens from the beetroot and save for juicing later. Cut the beetroot into quarters. Place a jug under the juicer's spout to collect the juice.
3. Feed each ingredient through the juicer's intake tube in the order listed.
4. When the juice stops flowing, remove the jug and stir the juice.
5. Serve immediately.

Cinnamon Berry and Gingered Spinach Juice
Prep time: 5 minutes | Cook time: 0 minutes | Serves 1

- 120g blueberries
- 160g spinach
- 1 cucumber
- Fresh ginger root
- ½ teaspoon maca powder
- ¼ teaspoon ground cinnamon

1. Wash the blueberries, spinach, cucumber, and ginger root.
2. Place a jug under the juicer's spout to collect the juice.
3. Feed the first four ingredients through the juicer's intake tube in the order listed.
4. When the juice stops flowing, remove the jug, add the maca powder and ground cinnamon, then stir.
5. Serve immediately.

Strawberry-Cucumber Juice
Prep time: 5 minutes | Cook time: 0 minutes | Serves 2

- 1 large cucumber, peeled, cut into chunks
- 6 fresh strawberries, hulled
- 2 medium carrots, peeled
- 1 large red apple, quartered

1. Wash the fruits and vegetables. Peel the cucumber and carrots.
2. Pass through a juicer along with strawberries and serve over ice cubes.

Kale Celery Fruity Juice
Prep time: 5 minutes | Cook time: 10 minutes | Serves 2

- 3 leaves kale
- 2 red plums
- 3 stalks celery
- 1 apple

1. Pit the plums and core the apples. Add to a juicer along with kale and celery.
2. Process and enjoy.

Apple Berry Juice
Prep time: 5 minutes | Cook time: 5 minutes | Serves 2

- 3 apples, cored
- 1 cup of cranberry juice
- 1 cup of fresh blueberries

1. Process the apples and blueberries through a juicer and pour into a jug.
2. Add the cranberry juice, stir well, and enjoy over ice.

Orange Pineapple Chili
Prep time: 5 minutes | Cook time: 5 minutes | Serves 2

- ½ pineapple
- ½ lime, peeled
- 7 medium carrots
- ½ small chili
- Remove the rind from the lime.

1. Trim the ends of carrots and discard the greens. Run through a juicer along with lime, pineapple, and chili.
2. Pour into a tall glass, add 2-3 cubes of ice and drink immediately.

Sweet Summer Quencher
Prep time: 5 minutes | Cook time: 10 minutes | Serves 2

- 4 large romaine leaves
- ½ cucumber
- 1 orange, peeled
- 1 cup strawberries
- 1 small apple
- 1 cup watermelon

1. Feed the ingredients one at a time, in the order listed, through the juicer.
2. Stir the juice and pour into glasses to serve.

Ginger Pear Celery Juice
Prep time: 5 minutes | Cook time: 5 minutes | Serves 2

- 5 celery stalks
- 2 pears
- 2.5 cm piece of fresh ginger root

1. Wash the pears and celery and cut into chunks. Pass through a juicer along with ginger.
2. Let sit for 2-5 minutes and enjoy.

Kale Orange Apple Green Juice
Prep time: 5 minutes | Cook time: 10 minutes | Serves 2

- 1 medium orange, peeled
- 3 kale leaves
- 1 medium apple, cut into wedges

1. Peel and cut the apple and orange. Add to a juicer along with kale leaves.
2. Pour the extracted juice into a glass and enjoy.

Grapefruit And Kohlrabi
Prep time: 5 minutes | Cook time: 10 minutes | Serves 2

- ¼ small kohlrabi
- ½ pink or red grapefruit, peeled
- 2 large celery stalks
- ½ apple

1. Feed the ingredients one at a time, in the order listed, through the juicer.
2. Stir the juice and pour into glasses to serve.

Strawberry Tomato Juice
Prep time: 5 minutes | Cook time: 5 minutes | Serves 2

- 3 ripe tomatoes, cut into quarters
- 2 cups of strawberries
- 2-3 basil leaves

1. Wash the strawberries, tomatoes and basil leaves and process through a juicer.
2. Pour into a glass over ice, garnish with a basil leaf and serve.

Chapter 8
Anti-Aging and Energizing Juices

Chocolate Caramel
Prep time: 5 minutes | Cook time: 5 minutes | Serves 1

- 1 tablespoon toasted almonds
- 3 tablespoons double cream
- 2 tablespoons Homemade Keto Caramel
- ½ cup water
- 1 tablespoon unsweetened cocoa powder
- 8 drops liquid stevia
- 1 teaspoon vanilla extract
- ¼ teaspoon instant coffee powder
- ⅛ teaspoon sea salt
- 1 cup ice cubes

1. Add the almonds to a blender and pulse until powdery.
2. Add the cream, Homemade Keto Caramel, water, cocoa powder, stevia, vanilla extract, instant coffee powder, and salt to the blender and process until smooth.
3. Add the ice cubes and pulse until thick and creamy, tamping down as necessary.
4. Pour into a glass and serve immediately.

Sweet Potato Orange
Prep time: 5 minutes | Cook time: 10 minutes| Serves 2

- 2 large kale leaves
- ½ small sweet potato, peeled
- 2 large Swiss chard leaves
- ¼ lemon
- 1 orange, peeled
- ½ large cucumber

1. Thoroughly wash all ingredients, cut, and run through a juicer.
2. Pour into a juicer and enjoy.

10 Minute Healthy Ulcer Care Drink
Prep time: 10 minutes | Cook time: 0 minutes | Serves 2

- 2 cups green cabbage
- 2 cups spinach
- 3 green chard leaves
- 3 celery ribs
- 1 green apple

1. Wash all the ingredients.
2. Cut the cabbage in half, then slice or chop into smaller pieces.
3. Trim the ends from the celery, then cut into 4-inch pieces.
4. Remove the apple core and discard. Cut the apple into quarters, leaving the peel intact.
5. Place a pitcher under the juicer's spout to collect the juice.
6. Feed each ingredient through the juicer's intake tube in the order listed.
7. When the juice stops flowing, remove the pitcher and stir the juice.
8. Serve immediately.

Milky Pistachio Juice

Prep time: 5 minutes | Cook time: 0 minutes | Serves 1

- ½ cup plain whole-milk Greek yogurt
- ½ cup unsweetened almond milk, plus more as needed
- Zest and juice of 1 lemon
- 1 tablespoon extra-virgin olive oil
- 1 tablespoon shelled pistachios, coarsely chopped
- 1 to 2 teaspoons agave syrup or honey (optional)
- ¼ to ½ teaspoon ground allspice or unsweetened pumpkin pie spice ¼ teaspoon ground cinnamon
- ¼ teaspoon vanilla extract

1. In a blender or a large wide-mouth jar, if using an immersion blender, combine the yogurt, ½ cup almond milk, lemon zest and juice, olive oil, pistachios, agave syrup or honey (if using), allspice, cinnamon, and vanilla and blend until smooth and creamy, adding more almond milk to achieve your desired consistency.

Cardamom spiced Coconut Juice

Prep time: 5 minutes | Cook time: 0 minutes | Serves 1

- 1 cup full-fat coconut milk
- 1 tablespoon coconut cream
- 1 teaspoon finely diced fresh ginger
- ½ teaspoon spirulina powder
- ¼ teaspoon ground cardamom
- ¼ teaspoon ground cinnamon
- 1 tablespoon vanilla protein powder
- 1 cup ice cubes
- 1 teaspoon flaxseed

1. In a high-powered blender, combine the coconut milk, coconut cream, ginger, spirulina, cardamom, and cinnamon.
2. Blend for 30 seconds. Add the protein powder and ice cubes, and blend on high for 1 minute.
3. Pour the juice into a glass, sprinkle the flaxseed on top, and enjoy.

Spinach Protein Juice

Prep time: 5 minutes | Cook time: 0 minutes | Serves 1

- 250g frozen spinach
- 240ml unsweetened almond milk
- 2 tablespoons hemp hearts
- 1 tablespoon MCT oil
- 1 scoop chocolate-flavored protein powder

1. Put all the ingredients in a blender and blend until smooth, 30 to 45 seconds. Pour into a glass and serve immediately.

Nutmeg Spiced Avocado Juice

Prep time: 5 minutes | Cook time: 0 minutes | Serves 2

- ⅓ ripe avocado, peeled and pitted
- 3 teaspoons cacao powder, unsweetened
- ¼ teaspoon grated nutmeg
- 2 teaspoons granulated erythritol
- 1 cup almond milk
- ½ cup water

1. Purée all ingredients in a blender until smooth and uniform. Spoon into two glasses and enjoy!

Sweet Dreams

Prep time: 5 minutes | Cook time: 10 minutes | Serves 2

- 1 large celery stalk
- ½ fennel bulb
- 1 cup strawberries
- 2 medium apples

1. Feed the ingredients one at a time, in the order listed, through the juicer.
2. Stir the juice and pour into glasses to serve.

Spring Has Sprung

Prep time: 5 minutes | Cook time: 10 minutes | Serves 2

- 12 asparagus spears
- 4-inch piece broccoli stem
- ½ lemon
- 1 apple

1. Feed the ingredients one at a time, in the order listed, through the juicer.
2. Stir the juice and pour into glasses to serve.

Minted Raspberry Cocktail
Prep time: 5 minutes | Cook time: 10 minutes | Serves 2

- 1 apple
- ½ lemon
- 1 cup raspberries
- 4 teaspoons fresh mint
- 1 large cucumber

1. Feed the ingredients one at a time, in the order listed, through the juicer.
2. Stir the juice and pour into glasses to serve.

Green Paradise
Prep time: 5 minutes | Cook time: 10 minutes | Serves 2

- 1 pear
- 4 stalks celery
- 2 stalks kale
- 1 cup spinach
- ½ lemon juice

1. Wash the greens, pear and lemon and cut into chunks. Then pass all ingredients through a juicer.
2. Pour into a glass and drink immediately.

Apple, Kohlrabi, And Kale Sipper
Prep time: 5 minutes | Cook time: 10 minutes | Serves 2

- 2 large celery stalks
- 2 kale leaves
- ¼ small kohlrabi
- ½ lime, peeled
- 2 apples

1. Feed the ingredients one at a time, in the order listed, through the juicer.
2. Stir the juice and pour into glasses to serve.

Plum Good
Prep time: 5 minutes | Cook time: 10 minutes | Serves 2

- 1 cup blackberries
- 2 black or red plums
- 8 small celery stalks

1. Feed the ingredients one at a time, in the order listed, through the juicer.
2. Stir the juice and pour into glasses to serve.

Ginger Beet and Tangy Celery Juice
Prep time: 5 minutes | **Cook time:** 0 minutes | **Serves** 2

- 1 medium golden or red beet
- 1 large yellow bell pepper
- 1-inch piece fresh ginger root
- ½ lemon
- 8 small celery stalks
- ½ large cucumber

1. Wash and chop the beet into small pieces.
2. Remove the stem and seeds from the bell pepper and chop into small pieces.
3. Peel and chop the ginger root.
4. Squeeze the juice from the half lemon and set aside.
5. Wash and chop the celery stalks into small pieces.
6. Peel and chop the cucumber.
7. In a juicer, feed the chopped ingredients one at a time in the order listed, collecting the juice in a container placed under the spout.
8. Stir the juice and pour into glasses to serve.

Asparagus Blended with Peppered Chard
Prep time: 5 minutes | **Cook time:** 0 minutes | **Serves** 2

- 8 asparagus spears
- 2 cups Swiss chard
- ½ lemon
- 1 orange, peeled
- ½ yellow bell pepper
- 1 large cucumber

1. Peel, cut, deseed, and/or chop the ingredients as needed.
2. Place a container under the juicer's spout.
3. Feed the ingredients one at a time, in the order listed, through the juicer.
4. Stir the juice and pour into glasses to serve.

Plum Cocktail
Prep time: 5 minutes | **Cook time:** 10 minutes | **Serves** 2

- 1 cup black or red grapes
- 2 black or red plums, ripe but still firm
- 1-inch piece fresh ginger root
- 1 medium red apple

1. Feed the ingredients one at a time, in the order listed, through the juicer.
2. Stir the juice and pour into glasses to serve.

Cruciferous Grapefruit Blend
Prep time: 5 minutes | Cook time: 10 minutes | Serves 2

- 2-inch piece broccoli stem
- ½ cup red cabbage
- ½ cup cauliflower
- 2 large carrots
- ½ pink or red grapefruit, peeled

1. Feed the ingredients one at a time, in the order listed, through the juicer.
2. Stir the juice and pour into glasses to serve.

Fine And Dandy
Prep time: 5 minutes | Cook time: 10 minutes | Serves 2

- 2.5 cm piece fresh turmeric root
- 5 cm piece broccoli stem
- 10 large dandelion leaves
- ½ fennel bulb
- 2 kale leaves
- ½ apple
- 1 orange, peeled
- ½ cucumber

1. Feed the ingredients one at a time, in the order listed, through the juicer.
2. Stir the juice and pour into glasses to serve.

Quick and Healthy Carrot Celery Juice
Prep time: 5 minutes | Cook time: 0 minutes | Serves 2

- 4 large carrots
- ½ lemon
- 6 large celery stalks

1. Peel, cut, deseed, and/or chop the ingredients as needed.
2. Place a container under the juicer's spout.
3. Feed the ingredients one at a time, in the order listed, through the juicer.
4. Stir the juice and pour into glasses to serve.

Tangy Celery and Chard with Pear
Prep time: 5 minutes | Cook time: 0 minutes | Serves 2

- 4 small celery stalks
- 4 small Swiss chard leaves
- 1 firm pear
- ½ lemon
- ½ large cucumber

1. Peel, cut, deseed, and/or chop the ingredients as needed.
2. Place a container under the juicer's spout.
3. Feed the ingredients one at a time, in the order listed, through the juicer.
4. Stir the juice and pour into glasses to serve.

Chapter 9
Structure Support

Morning Green Glory
Prep time: 5 minutes | Cook time: 10 minutes| Serves 2

- 10 kale leaves
- 2 large handfuls of spinach
- 6 romaine lettuce leaves
- 2 cucumbers
- 6 celery sticks
- 2 green apples
- 2 lemons

1. Wash and prepare the ingredients, and cut to size for your juicer.
2. Run through your juicer, then pour into a glass and enjoy.

Electrolyte Lemonade
Prep time: 5 minutes | Cook time: 10 minutes| Serves 2

- 120 ml coconut water
- ½ tablespoon fresh lemon juice
- 5 drops liquid stevia
- ⅛ teaspoon sea salt
- ⅛ teaspoon NoSalt Sodium-Free Salt
- 120 ml ice cubes

1. Stir all ingredients together in a glass.
2. Serve.

Cleanse Assist

Prep time: 5 minutes | Cook time: 10 minutes| Serves 2

- 480 ml kale
- 120 ml dandelion greens
- 1 pear
- ½ lemon

1. Wash all the ingredients.
2. Cut the pear into quarters, removing the core and seeds, but leaving the peel intact.
3. Peel the lemon half and cut into quarters.
4. Place a pitcher under the juicer's spout to collect the juice.
5. Feed each ingredient through the juicer's intake tube in the order listed.
6. When the juice stops flowing, remove the pitcher and stir the juice.
7. Serve immediately.

Ginger Blast

Prep time: 5 minutes | Cook time: 10 minutes| Serves 2

- 360 ml spinach
- 240 ml cherries, pitted
- Fresh ginger root
- 240 ml sparkling water

1. Wash the spinach, cherries, and ginger root.
2. Remove the cherry pits and stems.
3. Slice off a 2-inch piece of the ginger root.
4. Place a pitcher under the juicer's spout to collect the juice.
5. Feed each ingredient through the juicer's intake tube in the order listed.
6. When the juice stops flowing, remove the pitcher and stir the juice.
7. Serve immediately.

Immunity Plus
Prep time: 5 minutes | Cook time: 10 minutes| Serves 2

- 1 small beet
- 2 carrots
- 8 celery ribs
- 1 broccoli stem
- 2 garlic cloves, peeled

1. Wash all the ingredients except the garlic.
2. Remove any greens from the beet and save for juicing later. Cut the beet into quarters.
3. Trim the ends from the carrots and celery, then cut into 4-inch pieces.
4. Remove the stalk from the broccoli crown with a knife and discard or save to juice later. Cut the crown into small florets.
5. Place a pitcher under the juicer's spout to collect the juice.
6. Feed each ingredient through the juicer's intake tube in the order listed.
7. When the juice stops flowing, remove the pitcher and stir the juice.
8. Serve immediately.

Aloe Cleanser
Prep time: 5 minutes | Cook time: 10 minutes| Serves 2

- 30g alfalfa sprouts
- 1 pear
- 240g cabbage, chopped
- 60ml aloe vera juice

1. Wash the alfalfa sprouts, pear, and cabbage.
2. Cut the pear into quarters, removing the core and seeds, but leaving the peel intact.
3. Cut the cabbage in half, then slice or chop into smaller pieces.
4. Place a pitcher under the juicer's spout to collect the juice.
5. Feed the first three ingredients through the juicer's intake tube in the order listed.
6. When the juice stops flowing, remove the pitcher, add the aloe vera juice, and stir.
7. Serve immediately.

Good, Good, Good Digestion

Prep time: 5 minutes | Cook time: 10 minutes | Serves 2

- 240g papaya, chopped
- 6 kale leaves
- 1 small piece fresh turmeric root (about 2 cm)
- 1 lemon

1. Wash the kale, turmeric root, and lemon.
2. Cut the papaya in half lengthwise. Scoop out seeds and discard, then scoop out flesh and discard the papaya skin.
3. Slice off a 2-inch piece of the turmeric root.
4. Peel the lemon and cut into quarters.
5. Place a pitcher under the juicer's spout to collect the juice.
6. Feed each ingredient through the juicer's intake tube in the order listed.
7. When the juice stops flowing, remove the pitcher, and stir the juice.
8. Serve immediately.

Chlorophyll Boost

Prep time: 5 minutes | Cook time: 10 minutes | Serves 2

- 1 cup chopped pineapple
- 4 kale leaves, washed and chopped
- 1 cup spinach, washed
- 1/2 cucumber, chopped
- 7 fresh mint leaves
- 1/2 teaspoon spirulina powder

1. Wash the kale, spinach, cucumber, and mint.
2. Trim the ends and skin from the pineapple, then remove core and discard. Cut pineapple into 1-inch chunks.
3. Trim the ends from the cucumber, then cut into 4-inch pieces.
4. Place a pitcher under the juicer's spout to collect the juice.
5. Feed the first five ingredients through the juicer's intake tube in the order listed.
6. When the juice stops flowing, remove the pitcher, add the spirulina powder, and stir.
7. Serve immediately.

Epic Green Juice

Prep time: 5 minutes | Cook time: 10 minutes | Serves 2

- 1 medium turnip with greens, washed and chopped
- 1 pear, washed and chopped
- 1 cup spinach, washed
- 1/2 cucumber, chopped
- 1 cup chopped cantaloupe

1. Wash the turnip, pear, spinach, and cucumber.
2. Trim the greens and cut the turnip into small chunks.
3. Cut the pear into quarters, removing the core and seeds, but leaving the peel intact.
4. Trim the ends from the cucumber, then cut into 4-inch pieces.
5. Cut the rockmelon into quarters. Remove the rind, scoop out the seeds, and discard. Cut the rockmelon into small pieces.
6. Place a pitcher under the juicer's spout to collect the juice.
7. Feed each ingredient through the juicer's intake tube in the order listed.
8. When the juice stops flowing, remove the pitcher and stir the juice.
9. Serve immediately.

Apple and Pear Mint Juice

Prep time: 5 minutes | Cook time: 10 minutes | Serves 2

- 1 cucumber
- 4 red apples
- 4 pears
- 1 cup of fresh mint leaves

1. Wash the pears, apples, cucumber, and mint leaves.
2. Run all ingredients through a juicer and drink immediately.

Asparagus Apple and Celery Juice
Prep time: 15 minutes | Cook time: 0 minutes | Serves 1

- 6 asparagus spears
- 1 green apple
- 2 celery ribs
- ¼ cup filtered water

1. Wash the asparagus, apple, and celery.
2. Trim ½ inch from the bottom of the asparagus, then cut stalks into 4-inch pieces.
3. Remove the apple core and discard. Cut the apple into quarters, leaving the peel intact.
4. Place a pitcher under the juicer's spout to collect the juice.
5. When the juice stops flowing, remove the pitcher, add the filtered water, and stir the juice.
6. Serve immediately.

Orange Rabbit
Prep time: 5 minutes | Cook time: 10 minutes| Serves 2

- 4-inch piece broccoli stem
- 4 large carrots
- 1 orange, peeled
- 4 large celery stalks

1. Feed the ingredients one at a time, in the order listed, through the juicer.
2. Stir the juice and pour into glasses to serve.

I Dream Of Green
Prep time: 5 minutes | Cook time: 10 minutes| Serves 2

- 1 cup honeydew melon, chopped
- 4 collard green leaves, washed
- 3 cups cabbage, chopped
- 1 lemon, juiced

1. Wash the collard greens, cabbage, and lemon.
2. Cut the honeydew melon into quarters. Remove the rind and discard. Cut the melon into small pieces.
3. Cut the cabbage in half, then slice or chop into smaller pieces.
4. Peel the lemon and cut into quarters.
5. Place a pitcher under the juicer's spout to collect the juice.
6. Feed each ingredient through the juicer's intake tube in the order listed.
7. When the juice stops flowing, remove the pitcher and stir the juice.
8. Serve immediately.

Now And Zen Green Juice

Prep time: 5 minutes | Cook time: 10 minutes | Serves 2

- 2 kiwis
- 6 asparagus spears
- 4 celery ribs
- 4 kale leaves

1. Wash all the ingredients.
2. Peel the kiwis, then cut them into quarters. (There's no need to peel them unless you want to.)
3. Trim the bottoms of the asparagus, then cut into small pieces.
4. Trim the ends from the celery, then cut into 4-inch pieces.
5. Place a pitcher under the juicer's spout to collect the juice.
6. Feed each ingredient through the juicer's intake tube in the order listed.
7. When the juice stops flowing, remove the pitcher and stir the juice.
8. Serve immediately.

Emerald Alkalizing Juice

Prep time: 5 minutes | Cook time: 10 minutes | Serves 2

- 3 cups spinach
- 1 red apple
- ½ cucumber
- ¼ cup filtered water
- ½ tablespoon wheatgrass powder
- 1 tablespoon apple cider vinegar

1. Wash the spinach, apple, and cucumber.
2. Remove the apple core and discard. Cut the apple into quarters, leaving the peel intact.
3. Trim the ends from the cucumber, then cut into 4-inch pieces.
4. Place a pitcher under the juicer's spout to collect the juice.
5. Feed the first three ingredients through the juicer's intake tube in the order listed.
6. When the juice stops flowing, remove the pitcher, add the water, wheatgrass powder and apple cider vinegar, and stir the juice.
7. Serve immediately.

Chapter 10
Immune Boosting Juices

Limey Orange and Cucumber Juice

Prep time: 15 minutes | Cook time: 0 minutes | Serves 1

- 2 cups mixed greens
- 1 orange
- 1 cucumber
- ½ lime
- 1 teaspoon maca powder

1. Wash the mixed greens, orange, cucumber, and lime.
2. Peel the orange and lime, then cut into quarters.
3. Place a pitcher under the juicer's spout to collect the juice.
4. Feed the first four ingredients through the juicer's intake tube in the order listed.
5. When the juice stops flowing, remove the pitcher, add the maca powder, and stir the juice.
6. Serve immediately.

Vitamin C Celebration

Prep time: 5 minutes | Cook time: 10 minutes | Serves 2

- 1 orange
- 1/2 red bell pepper, seeded and chopped
- 1 cup broccoli florets
- 2 collard green leaves
- 1/4 cucumber, chopped

1. Wash all the ingredients.
2. Peel the orange and cut into quarters.
3. Remove the stem and seeds from the bell pepper. Cut into small pieces.
4. Remove the stalk from the broccoli crown with a knife and discard or save to juice later. Cut the crown into small florets.
5. Trim the ends from the cucumber, then cut into quarters.
6. Place a pitcher under the juicer's spout to collect the juice.
7. Feed each ingredient through the juicer's intake tube in the order listed.
8. When the juice stops flowing, remove the pitcher and stir the juice.
9. Serve immediately.

Berry Good
Prep time: 5 minutes | Cook time: 10 minutes| Serves 2

- 2 large bok choy stems
- 2 cups spinach
- 1 cup strawberries
- Handful cilantro
- ½ lemon

1. Feed the ingredients one at a time, in the order listed, through the juicer.
2. Stir the juice and pour into glasses to serve.

Walk In The Park
Prep time: 5 minutes | Cook time: 10 minutes| Serves 2

- ½ fennel bulb
- 2 large kale leaves
- 1 apple
- 1 large cucumber

1. Feed the ingredients one at a time, in the order listed, through the juicer.
2. Stir the juice and pour into glasses to serve.

Orange Potato Bliss
Prep time: 5 minutes | Cook time: 10 minutes| Serves 2

- 1- to 2-inch piece fresh turmeric root
- 1 large cucumber
- 1 small sweet potato, peeled
- 2 oranges, peeled
- 4 large celery stalks

1. Feed the ingredients one at a time, in the order listed, through the juicer.
2. Stir the juice and pour into glasses to serve.

Call Me Sweetheart
Prep time: 5 minutes | Cook time: 10 minutes| Serves 2

- Handful spinach
- 2 kiwifruit
- 1 small lime, peeled
- 1 cup pineapple
- 1 cup watermelon
- 4 small celery stalks

1. Feed the ingredients one at a time, in the order listed, through the juicer.
2. Stir the juice and pour into glasses to serve.

Lemony Red Velvet
Prep time: 10 minutes | Cook time: 0 minutes | Serves 1

- 2 medium apples 4 medium carrots ¼ small red cabbage ½ thumb ginger root 4 handfuls of spinach ½ lemon (peeled for a less bitter taste)

1. Thoroughly wash the fruits and vegetables.
2. Put them through a juicer and enjoy.

Super Detox Juice
Prep time: 10 minutes | Cook time: 0 minutes | Serves 1

- 4 carrots
- 3 apples
- 2 celery stalks
- 1 cup of spinach
- 1 chunk of ginger

1. Put all ingredients through the juicer.
2. Add Ice.
3. Enjoy

Spinach with Purple Pineapple
Prep time: 10 minutes | Cook time: 0 minutes | Serves 2

- 250g red cabbage
- Handful of spinach
- 250g pineapple
- 2 Cara or other small oranges, peeled

1. Peel, cut, deseed, and/or chop the ingredients as needed.
2. Place a container under the juicer's spout.
3. Feed the ingredients in the order listed, through the juicer.
4. Alternate ingredients, finishing with the orange or the pineapple.
5. Stir the juice and pour into glasses to serve.

Heavenly Kale
Prep time: 5 minutes | Cook time: 10 minutes| Serves 2

- 2 large kale leaves
- 1 cup pineapple
- 2 cups watermelon

1. Feed the ingredients one at a time, in the order listed, through the juicer.
2. Stir the juice and pour into glasses to serve.

Brainy Cooler
Prep time: 5 minutes | Cook time: 10 minutes| Serves 2

- 1 cup blueberries
- ½ small lime, peeled
- 2 cups watermelon, with rind if organic
- 5 to 6 large green or purple basil leaves
- ½ medium cucumber

1. Feed the ingredients one at a time, in the order listed, through the juicer.
2. Stir the juice and pour into glasses to serve.

Swiss Plum
Prep time: 5 minutes | Cook time: 10 minutes| Serves 2

- 2 large celery stalks
- 4 medium Swiss chard leaves
- 2 black or red plums
- Handful parsley
- ½ cucumber

1. Feed the ingredients one at a time, in the order listed, through the juicer.
2. Stir the juice and pour into glasses to serve.

Tummy Tamer
Prep time: 5 minutes | Cook time: 10 minutes| Serves 2

- 2 large celery sticks
- ½ cup spinach
- 1 cup papaya
- ½ firm pear
- ½-inch piece fresh ginger root
- 4 parsley sprigs
- 1 large cucumber
- ¼ cup fresh coconut water

1. Pass each ingredient through a juicer in the order listed.
2. Stir the juice and pour into glasses to serve.

Appendix 1 Measurement Conversion Chart

Volume Equivalents (Dry)	
US STANDARD	METRIC (APPROXIMATE)
1/8 teaspoon	0.5 mL
1/4 teaspoon	1 mL
1/2 teaspoon	2 mL
3/4 teaspoon	4 mL
1 teaspoon	5 mL
1 tablespoon	15 mL
1/4 cup	59 mL
1/2 cup	118 mL
3/4 cup	177 mL
1 cup	235 mL
2 cups	475 mL
3 cups	700 mL
4 cups	1 L

Weight Equivalents	
US STANDARD	METRIC (APPROXIMATE)
1 ounce	28 g
2 ounces	57 g
5 ounces	142 g
10 ounces	284 g
15 ounces	425 g
16 ounces (1 pound)	455 g
1.5 pounds	680 g
2 pounds	907 g

Volume Equivalents (Liquid)		
US STANDARD	US STANDARD (OUNCES)	METRIC (APPROXIMATE)
2 tablespoons	1 fl.oz.	30 mL
1/4 cup	2 fl.oz.	60 mL
1/2 cup	4 fl.oz.	120 mL
1 cup	8 fl.oz.	240 mL
1 1/2 cup	12 fl.oz.	355 mL
2 cups or 1 pint	16 fl.oz.	475 mL
4 cups or 1 quart	32 fl.oz.	1 L
1 gallon	128 fl.oz.	4 L

Temperatures Equivalents	
FAHRENHEIT(F)	CELSIUS(C) APPROXIMATE)
225 °F	107 °C
250 °F	120 ° °C
275 °F	135 °C
300 °F	150 °C
325 °F	160 °C
350 °F	180 °C
375 °F	190 °C
400 °F	205 °C
425 °F	220 °C
450 °F	235 °C
475 °F	245 °C
500 °F	260 °C

Appendix 2 The Dirty Dozen and Clean Fifteen

The Environmental Working Group (EWG) is a nonprofit, nonpartisan organization dedicated to protecting human health and the environment Its mission is to empower people to live healthier lives in a healthier environment. This organization publishes an annual list of the twelve kinds of produce, in sequence, that have the highest amount of pesticide residue-the Dirty Dozen-as well as a list of the fifteen kinds ofproduce that have the least amount of pesticide residue-the Clean Fifteen.

THE DIRTY DOZEN	
The 2016 Dirty Dozen includes the following produce. These are considered among the year's most important produce to buy organic:	
Strawberries	Spinach
Apples	Tomatoes
Nectarines	Bell peppers
Peaches	Cherry tomatoes
Celery	Cucumbers
Grapes	Kale/collard greens
Cherries	Hot peppers
The Dirty Dozen list contains two additional itemskale/collard greens and hot peppers-because they tend to contain trace levels of highly hazardous pesticides.	

THE CLEAN FIFTEEN	
The least critical to buy organically are the Clean Fifteen list. The following are on the 2016 list:	
Avocados	Papayas
Corn	Kiw
Pineapples	Eggplant
Cabbage	Honeydew
Sweet peas	Grapefruit
Onions	Cantaloupe
Asparagus	Cauliflower
Mangos	
Some of the sweet corn sold in the United States are made from genetically engineered (GE) seedstock. Buy organic varieties of these crops to avoid GE produce.	

Appendix 3 Index

A

all-purpose flour 50, 53
allspice 15
almond 5, 14
ancho chile 10
ancho chile powder 5
apple 9
apple cider vinegar 9
arugula 51
avocado 11

B

bacon 52
balsamic vinegar 7, 12, 52
basil 5, 8, 11, 13
beet 52
bell pepper 50, 51, 53
black beans 50, 51
broccoli 51, 52, 53
buns 52
butter 50

C

canola oil 50, 51, 52
carrot 52, 53
cauliflower 5, 52
cayenne 5, 52
cayenne pepper 52
Cheddar cheese 52
chicken 6
chili powder 50, 51
chipanle pepper 50
chives 5, 6, 52
cinnamon 15
coconut 6
Colby Jack cheese 51
coriander 52
corn 50, 51
corn kernels 50
cumin 5, 10, 15, 50, 51, 52

D

diced panatoes 50
Dijon mustard 7, 12, 13, 51
dry onion powder 52

E

egg 14, 50, 53
enchilada sauce 51

F

fennel seed 53
flour 50, 53
fresh chives 5, 6, 52
fresh cilantro 52
fresh cilantro leaves 52
fresh dill 5
fresh parsley 6, 52
fresh parsley leaves 52

G

garlic 5, 9, 10, 11, 13, 14, 50, 51, 52, 53
garlic powder 8, 9, 52, 53

H

half-and-half 50
hemp seeds 8
honey 9, 51

I

instant rice 51

K

kale 14
kale leaves 14
ketchup 53
kosher salt 5, 10, 15

L

lemon 5, 6, 14, 51, 53
lemon juice 6, 8, 11, 13, 14, 51
lime 9, 12
lime juice 9, 12
lime zest 9, 12

M

maple syrup 7, 12, 53
Marinara Sauce 5
micro greens 52
milk 5, 50
mixed berries 12
Mozzarella 50, 53
Mozzarella cheese 50, 53
mushroom 51, 52
mustard 51, 53
mustard powder 53

N

nutritional yeast 5

O

olive oil 5, 12, 13, 14, 50, 51, 52, 53
onion 5, 50, 51
onion powder 8
oregano 5, 8, 10, 50

P

panatoes 50, 52
paprika 5, 15, 52
Parmesan cheese 51, 53
parsley 6, 52
pesto 52
pink Himalayan salt 5, 7, 8, 11
pizza dough 50, 53
pizza sauce 50
plain coconut yogurt 6
plain Greek yogurt 5
porcini powder 53
potato 53

R

Ranch dressing 52
raw honey 9, 12, 13
red pepper flakes 5, 8, 14, 15, 51, 53
ricotta cheese 53

S

saffron 52
Serrano pepper 53
sugar 10
summer squash 51

T

tahini 5, 8, 9, 11
thyme 50
toasted almonds 14
tomato 5, 50, 52, 53
turmeric 15

U

unsalted butter 50
unsweetened almond milk 5

V

vegetable broth 50
vegetable stock 51

W

white wine 8, 11
wine vinegar 8, 10, 11

Y

yogurt 5, 6

Z

zucchini 50, 51, 52, 53

SUMMER G. FLORES

Printed in Great Britain
by Amazon